Scooters!

The ULTIMATE guide to
the COOLEST Ride

Jeremy Case

Illustrated by Zac Sandler

First Aladdin Paperbacks edition May 2001

Text copyright © 2000 by Jeremy Case
Illustrations copyright © 2000 by Zac Sandler

Aladdin Paperbacks
An imprint of Simon & Schuster
Children's Publishing Division
1230 Avenue of the Americas
New York, NY 10020

Originally published in England in paperback by Penguin Books Ltd. under the title Scootermania: Everything you need to know about Scooters.

Designed by Dan Newman/Perfect Bound

Printed and bound in the United States of America

2 4 6 8 10 9 7 5 3 1

CIP Data for this book is available from the Library of Congress.

ISBN 0-689-84529-4

82260

Contents

We Have Kickoff!

When the shiny, sleek, lightweight scooter arrived in the U.S. in winter 1999, many people wrote it off as just another craze. Newspapers and magazines described it as "another Furby" and "the new yo-yo," thinking that the fad would pass as soon as the gleam on the aluminum wore off. How wrong they were.

> **"It's the most fun I've had not on a surfboard."**
> *Simon, 28, Razor*

Updated for the millennium, the scooter has taken the globe by storm. Kids are using them for fun, adults are riding them to work, and their popularity shows no sign of fading. At present they're selling at a rate of 300,000 a week worldwide.

The appeal of the scooter—apart from its hugely stylish design—is that it's as light as a laptop, can be folded up quickly, and fits into a backpack. You can carry it with you wherever you go—to the park, on the subway, or even to a fancy restaurant. It's ideal for short journeys of can't-be-bothered-to-walk length.

Unlike with bikes, there's no problem with security, as you don't have to lock it up to a flimsy drainpipe. Unlike with skateboards, you're much less likely to fall off. And unlike with in-line skates, you don't have to waste time putting them on and taking them off. The scooter's ready to roll in two ticks and three clicks.

"Love it. Everyone I've met says it's supercool and awesome and where can they buy one."
Daniel, 17, Razor

Scooters are ideal for this environmentally aware, exercise-obsessed, time-is-money age. People are using them instead of driving or jumping on a bus, and they're getting a workout at the same time. It's exercise without the hassle. On flat ground, you can scoot about as fast as you can run (but with far less go-go juice), and on hills you can glide down with the minimum of effort. When you get to the bottom, if you don't want to push up the other side, you can just pick up your machine and walk.

"A lot of people at school had them, and they're great fun. I can do wheelies, and it only takes me five minutes to get to school, rather than ten."
Edward, 10, Razor

As if they weren't cool enough already, scooters have been given an added dose of kudos by a whole A-list of celebrities. In New York, Oscar-winner Kevin Spacey rode his electric scooter onto the set of David Letterman's talk show and declared it the only way to get around.

In cities, parents are getting kids to school on them.

In a Wal-Mart in England, the staff was supplied with scooters to help them get around the huge shop floors. Executives use them to whiz through the city traffic to meetings. And moms and dads who've bought them for their kids soon find they're "borrowing" the scooters themselves to pop down to the store for a carton of milk.

> **"It goes fast and has cool wheels."**
> *Rosie, 7, Razor*

On college campuses the Razor name has become as famous as Nike and Microsoft. At motor-racing circuits, pit crews use motorized Go-Peds for running errands. In the Helsinki airport, luggage porters zip around on specially customized models built to carry heavy suitcases.

Here in the U.S., Internet companies stage races across warehouse-style offices, Razors being the essential piece of equipment for any self-respecting dotcom entrepreneur. In film studios staff use them to get between sets. Even former skateboarders have been converted and are now using them to do tricks. And in parks the world over, kids ride them, well, simply because they're fun.

> **"This is the best toy I've had my hands on in ages."**
> *Nicky, 26, Razor*

super models

From scooters you can buy at the mall to ones you can only dream about—they're all here. Remember, it takes all types.

PUSH POWER–Get a Kick out of These!
THE RAZOR SCOOTER

Known as the Micro in Europe, this stylish machine was the first push scooter to arrive on the modern scene and launched a whole chasing pack of copycats. The Swiss-designed, Chinese-produced Razor is still the most popular, thanks to its patented folding mechanism, durability—the heat treatment on the aluminum makes it stronger—and for its get-around-town cool.

The slightly more pricey Razor B1 comes with a rear wheel cover that prevents splatters and serves as a friction brake, 4-inch wheels, ABEC-5 bearings and tough shocks. The wheels and the handlebars are color coordinated.

SPECS
- aircraft-grade aluminum foldable frame
- rear-wheel guard brake
- 4 in. polyurethane wheels
- clip-on shoulder strap
- multiclip for hanging bags, etc.
- weight: 6.07 lbs. Micro Pro: 7.04 lbs.

"I like it because it becomes little."
Enrique, 12, Razor

If you liked this, you'll like:
the new Razors—the Air and Air Flex (see p. 82).

Web site:
www.razorusa.com
www.waizit.com
www.push-scooters.com

THE JD BUG

Leading contender from the huge army of Razor imitators, mainly because it was actually brought out by the same company. More gimmicky than the original and with a crazy slogan ("Step on, bug out"), it comes in five colors—orange, blue, red, green, and black—and you can mix and match the wheels, grip tape, straps, and handlebars. Otherwise it's almost identical to the Razor, except that it has an extra inch on the footplate, which now finishes alongside the rear axle to give the back end of the scooter a bit more oomph.

SPECS
- same as the Micro, but with matching colored strap

If you liked this, you'll like:
the Viza Kikit (see p. 69).
Web site:
www.jdbugrazorscooter.com

❝Our house has three, and all my friends are getting them. Wow! We just love them, especially the new bright colors.❞
Alexandra, 12, JD Bug

THE KNOW-PED

Californian gas-scooter experts Go-Ped's only foot-powered machine is more old-school and less high-tech than the Razors, like a step back in time to the hippie sixties. The wider board and extra front brake, along with a wheel mechanism that just screams out for BMX-style stunt pegs, all mean that the Know-Ped's not only more suitable for longer trips than the Micro, but it's just peachy for performing tricks. Especially in those colors—Flaming Yellow, Ferrari Red, and Beach Boy Blue. A real good-time scooter.

If you liked this, you'll like: the antique one you'll find in your parents' attic.
Web sites:
www.goped.com/Home.html
www.landsurfing.com/pushped.html

SPECS
- aircraft-quality high-carbon steel foldable frame
- front caliper and rear-wheel spoon fender brake
- 6 in. nonpneumatic natural rubber wheels
- weight: 11.99 lbs.

THE K2 KICKBOARD

The only scooter that should be ridden sideways, the three-wheeled Kickboard is designed for the PlayStation generation with a joystick for steering. Just push it left or right and lean the bend-tastic board, and the two front wheels will track around to where you want to go. Hopefully. Plus, the bend in the board gives you a far smoother ride. This cross between a skateboard and a scooter costs a few bucks more, but it's by far the coolest machine on the market, a serious West Coast skater's piece of equipment for surfing the urban landscape, built for trendsetters who've never grown out of their boarding sneakers. Customize with either downhill tires, for Formula One speed freaks, or off-road wheels, for cross-country rally drivers (see p. 54).

If you liked this, you'll like: the K2 Carveboard, a four-wheeled, sloping-decked monster (see p. 82).

Web site: www.kickboard.de

SPECS
- injection-molded aluminum foldable frame
- springy wood/fiberglass deck
- three 4 in. polyurethane smoke wheels
- rear-wheel guard brake
- weight: 7.04 lbs.

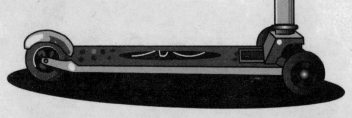

GAS POWER—For "Big Kids" Only

THE SPORT GO-PED

If you're the lazy type who likes to feel the wind in your hair, this is the baby for you. Find a bit of wasteland and you'll be burning rubber—with a few modifications, you can even get the speed up to more than thirty miles per hour. (If you think you're really cruising, why not enter the world championship races held in California?) The Sport boasts several world records, including "the greatest power-to-weight ratio of any transportation device in the world." But all you need to know is that it's the ultimate toy for today's urban warrior. The convertible sports car of the scooter world.

SPECS
- 22.5 cc engine
- max speed: 20 mph
- range: 25–30 miles
- foldable frame
- front caliper and rear-wheel guard brakes
- 6 in. nonpneumatic natural rubber wheels
- weight: 19.8 lbs.

If you liked this, you'll like: the Hoverboard, Go-Ped's first electric model, the scooter that feels like it's really hovering.
Web site: www.goped.com/Home.htm

9

ELECTRIC POWER–Charge Up, Charge Off

THE CITYBUG

The scooter for grown-ups, the sleek CityBug's advantage over your basic moped is its weight and foldability, plus the fact that you can recharge it from any old electric outlet. "It's designed for short, exhilarating trips into work," says spokesman Steve Malkin. "You can drive it through the office right up to your desk if the boss isn't watching." The Bug boasts a seat, real brakes, and, bizarrely, teeny pedals on the front wheel, which are only just larger than your big toe. However, the only exercise you're likely to get is building up your biceps lugging it around.

SPECS
- 150-watt motor; battery life one hour, rechargeable in five
- max speed: 15 mph
- range: 12 miles
- bicycle lamps
- 20 in. pneumatic wheels
- weight: 46.2 lbs.

If you liked this, you'll like:
a Vespa or the surely imminent Sinclair C5 revival.
Web site: www.citybug.com

"It's fab!"
Emma, 26, CityBug

PLAIN WEIRD—Scooters from Outer Space

SPECS
- high-tension steel frame
- 20.32 in. front wheel
- 3.12 in. polyurethane rear wheels
- weight: 30.8 lbs.

THE CALIFORNIA GRAND CHARIOT

It looks like the result of a nasty accident between a BMX and a couple of skateboards, and brings back memories of that tricycle you used to have when you were three, but one thing's for sure—if you scooted down the street on this, you'd certainly turn a few heads. In fact, you'd probably give a few people whiplash. Comes in black and blue, which are the colors you'll be if you keep getting confused about what it is exactly that you're riding. It looks like a holdover from the Roman Empire. But if you've seen *Ben Hur* and think of yourself as a gladiator, this is the only way to get around this A.D.

If you liked this, you'll like: Sorry, we just can't figure you guys out.

Web site:
www.beachcomber.com/Gadget/Fun/chariot.html
www.unmall.com/aus/kid_genius/g10_lg.html

THE KICKBIKE SPORT CLASSIC

Straight out of Finland, this half bike was created in the early nineties by medical student and world kick-sled champion Hannu Vierikko so he could train over the summer. Now kick-biking itself has gathered momentum and become an international sport in its own right, especially in Germany, Finland, the U.S., the Czech Republic, and Holland, where they hold regular events, including marathons. To prove what his contraption could do, or maybe just to show off, Vierikko himself rode 437 miles across the Rockies in 1998 in a week, reaching speeds of sixty miles per hour downhill. But no longer is it

seen as just a training tool for endurance athletes—it has recently become popular with couriers in Europe, is big on U.S. college campuses, and has just hit the streets of New York. It's cheaper than a bike and costs less to replace if stolen; has few moving parts to maintain and no greasy gears, so you won't get your shoelaces stuck in the chain, plus dismounting is easier than falling off a log. It may look like something your granddad used to wobble around on, but twelve thousand fans worldwide can't be wrong.

If you liked this, you'll like: the Dirt Surfer—not technically a scooter, as it has no handlebars, but a wicked piece of equipment nonetheless, like a thin metal longboard with BMX wheels (**www.ep-x.com/dirtsurfer**).
Web site: www.kickbike.com

SPECS
- steel frame
- standard road-bike front wheel
- 18.28 in. rear wheel
- high-pressure, puncture-resistant tires
- bicycle brakes
- weight: 19.8 lbs.

"The Kickbike is a gas. It's a lot of fun to play with."
Tom, 36, Kickbike

Other Makes Cluttering Up Store Shelves Around the World

Foot-Powered

* Blade Runner, Bulldog, California Chariot, E Shock, Exit Street Scooter, HCF-501 Foot Mini Scooter, Kick In-line Scooter, Mini Scooter Rollerboard, Mi3, 900R TT, Quickstep Mini Scooter, Racer, Razor Rollerboard Scooter, Rock Voxa, Rollerway, Skoooch, Stickboard, Tamitalos Fashion Scooter, Twister, Viza Kikit, Xootr Comp, Xootr Cruz, Xootr Street

Gas-Powered

* BigFoot, Blata Blatino Buzz Board, Go-Quad, Liquimatic, Swift, Viza Cruze, Viza Venom and Viza Viper (both with optional snow attachments, including a front ski and solid studded rear wheel!), X-Ped

Electric-Powered

* EMX Custom Model, EMX Racer, Four-Wheel Electric Leisure Scooter, Hoverboard, Two-Wheel Electric Leisure Scooter, Zappy Electric-Powered Scooter, Zappy Mobility, Zip Electric Scooter

CeLeBRiTY RiDeRS

The rich and famous are abandoning their chauffeur-driven limousines in favor of a healthier way of getting around between photo shoots and recording studios. Here are just some of the sightings:

On Push Scooters

* Robbie Williams, Prince Harry, Harrison Ford, Keith Flint (from The Prodigy), Ewan McGregor, Sarah Jessica Parker, Reef, Jude Law, Kirk Douglas, Jean Paul Gaultier, and Creed

On Motorized Scooters

* Boyzone, Jennifer Love Hewitt, and Kevin Spacey

SPIN DOCTOR

Like in-line skating and skateboarding, scooting is a blast. But even on those tiny wheels you can zip around at top speed, so you need to take care and show some respect for all the people around you. Follow these guidelines and soon you'll be scooting like a real pro.

✱ Wear the same safety gear as you would on a bike. A helmet and knee and elbow pads will protect you if you go for a tumble, especially if you're trying new tricks.

✖ **Make sure the handlebars are at the right height—and use them for steering, not leaning on, lazybones. One jolt and you'll go right over the top. You should stand up straight, with your weight on the back wheel—that way it's easier to steer, too. If you're bending over all the time, you'll end up walking around like a gibbon when you're older.**

✱ Use your scooter in parks and wide-open spaces. Busy areas are no fun anyway because you'll have to keep stopping all the time. Anywhere with plenty of room and a smooth surface is ideal. If you have to, scoot on the sidewalk, but *never* on the road.

✖ **Push off the first time on a flat, crack-free area. Your scooter will tackle bumps with ease once you've got some speed, but you may go flying if there's no momentum. If you're on the sidewalk, aim for the middle of the slabs so you don't spin out in the cracks.**

17

✱ When you're scooting, it's easy to end up staring at your feet all the time. Don't fall into this trap— make sure you look up and around for any looming obstacles or innocent pedestrians minding their own business.

✖ **Watch yourself in the rain. Brakes become less efficient and are liable to slip.**

✱ Keep your foot on the brake when you're going downhill or around a curve. You never know what's around that corner.

HOT TIPS

✱ Swap legs as soon as one starts getting tired. If you always use the same foot to push with, you'll end up with one thigh three times bigger than the other and your pants won't fit you anymore.

✖ **Don't use the skateboarding/surfing stance and do the sideways thang. Stand with your foot pointed forward and in the center of the deck for stability and balance. Not only is it bad for you to twist your body, but it looks weird too.**

✱ You've heard of tennis elbow, well now there's a new condition called **scootist's shin**. When you get off your scooter and pick it up, be very careful: the little fella's base will often spin around and give you a nasty whack on the shin. And bruised legs are *so* not a cool look.

✪ Wear a backpack to carry your stuff in and to put your scooter in when you're not using it.

✱ If you've got a cell phone, don't answer it while you're on the move. You'll fall off and embarrass yourself.

CARE

✪ Keep an eye out for bald patches on the back wheel if you do a lot of tricks. The brake wears down the plastic, and you won't be able to stop as well. If you use your scooter regularly, the wheels will probably have to be replaced every three months. But that's okay, because you can get some funky new ones in different colors (see p. 53 — Accessories).

✱ Keep the moving parts well oiled, especially if you've been out in the rain.

✪ Polish your scooter regularly to maintain that straight-outta-the-box gleam.

✱ It's not just your scooter that needs looking after. If you're always forgetting to swap pushing feet, you'll wear down the sole on one of your shoes much quicker than the other, and unless you buy a new pair of sneakers every three months, you'll end up walking around with a bizarre kind of limp.

People Who Would Be a Little Wobbly on a Scooter

❌ **Kenny** from *South Park* (in fact, anyone from *South Park*, seeing as they don't have any legs)

❌ **Godzilla** (not sure he could fit his foot on the board)

❌ **Long John Silver** (obviously)

❌ **Joey** from *Dawson's Creek* (all that emotional baggage wouldn't be good for balance)

❌ Any of the **Teletubbies** (they're not exactly streamlined, are they?)

❌ **Tiger Woods** (he'd fall in that pothole in one)

People Who Would Be Awesome on a Scooter

✱ **Mia Hamm** (she's got great feet)

✱ **Harry Potter** (he'd love a spell on a scooter)

✱ **Prince William** (to get around the endless marble-covered corridors of Buckingham Palace, and he could borrow his little brother's)

✱ **Stuart Little** (although he might have to lower the handlebars)

✱ **Bart Simpson** (obviously)

✱ **Buzz Lightyear** (because he can go to infinity and beyond)

TRICKS OF THE TRADE

All you need is a scooter, safety gear, lots of space, and a crowd of admirers.

If it takes you a while to get the hang of these stunts, don't worry. Skateboarders spend most of their time falling off and everyone still thinks they're cool.

Make sure you read the Spin Doctor's safety tips (p. 16) before you start!

All self-respecting scootists should have these tricks up their sleeve.

THE MANUAL

Your good old-fashioned wheelie, called a Manual on a scooter because you have no pedals. While either moving or standing still, put your weight at the rear of the scooter and lift up the front wheels using the handlebars.

Difficulty rating: ✖

THE CROUCH

Lower the handlebars as far as they'll go, give yourself
a push, and then get down on your haunches. Turn your
body slightly sideways to squeeze both feet onto
the scooter, and bingo! Low-bridge hassles are a thing
of the past.

Difficulty rating: ✱✱

THE BONUS

Perfect for negotiating a step up without even breaking your stride. Just before reaching it, push down on the ground with your foot, and lift up the handlebars.

Difficulty rating: ✖✖

THE TWO-WHEELER

This one's exclusive to the Kickboard. Stand on one side and lean in the opposite direction. Lift one of the front wheels off the ground and make like a pavement James Bond. Not to be attempted in a narrow alleyway, as you'll veer off into the wall.

Difficulty rating: ✖✖✖

THE HANDS-OFF

Build up a lot of speed, lean against the handlebar with your body, and just let go. Practice by taking one hand off at a time until you've mastered it. You're the king of the world!

Difficulty rating: ✳✳✳

THE FEET-OFF

You'll need better balancing skills than a performing sea lion, but it can be done. Build up some speed, tuck the handlebar into your midriff, and lift yourself up, sticking your legs out to either side of the T. Don't try to combine it with the Hands-off, though.

Difficulty rating: ✖✖✖✖

THE OLLIE

1

Skateboard classic invented by fourteen-year-old Alan "Ollie" Gelfand a whopping twenty-two years ago. Basically a jump while moving. Bend your knees and push down on the scooter (easier if you're on a springy Kickboard) to propel yourself up in the air. Requires a bit of mastering—poor old Ollie used to get his shoes and boards stolen by jealous skaters who thought he was using glue to stick his feet down.

Difficulty rating: ✳✳✳✳

2

3

29

THE ENDO

A reverse Manual—you lift the back wheel off the ground. Much easier on a Know-Ped, thanks to the front brake, but still possible on a Razor if you stand toward the front, jump slightly so there's no weight on the scooter, and push the handlebars forward at the same time. Don't push too hard though, or your face will become best friends with Mr. Asphalt.

Difficulty rating: ✳✳✳✳✳

Keep this up and you'll qualify for the scooting Olympics.

THE ONE-FOOT AIR

More of a skate-park trick, because it's easier if you launch yourself off a ramp. When you're airborne, grab hold of the board with one hand and stick the opposite leg out. It can be done on flat ground, mid-Ollie, but you'll need faster feet than Marion Jones.

Difficulty rating: ✶✶✶✶✶✶

THE GRIND

Another old skateboard favorite. Ollie up onto a step and then slide along it for as long as you can hold your balance, before peeling off and back into your stride. Don't worry, you're not cheating if you use your foot to push yourself back down—this is hard enough with four wheels, let alone two.

Difficulty rating: ✱✱✱✱✱✱

33

THE BUNNY HOP

They used to say BMX boys had all the fun, but now it's the revenge of the scootist. Do a Manual and with one foot on the rear brake, make like a pogo stick and bounce up and down on the back wheel. If that's not enough, you can either swap feet midjump, bounce around in a circle (known as a Brake Pivot), or spin the handlebars. Do all three at once and you're a scooting legend.

Difficulty rating: ✳✳✳✳✳✳✳

THE HANDLEBAR REVERSE

You thought handlebars were just for turning? Fool. If you're bombing along fast enough, you'll be able to flick them around so fast (so that the grip in your left hand is now in your right) that you'll still keep going in a straight line. Don't try it on a Know-Ped, though—you'll get all tangled up in the front brake cable and end up on the ground with those "tweet tweet" things circling above your head. Like in cartoons.

Difficulty rating: ✭✭✭✭✭✭✭✭

THE CHERRY PICKER

1

From the BMX stable. Standing still, wrap one leg around the stem and put that foot back onto the scooter so you're facing the wrong way with the handlebars in front of you. Swap your hands over and then move the same foot around again to return to where you started.

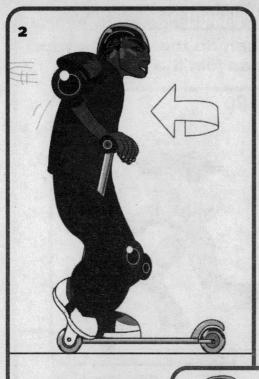

2

3

If you've got a Know-Ped, attach stunt pegs to the front wheel to stand on like a true BMXer. Like going for a spin without even moving.

Difficulty rating:
✱✱✱✱✱✱✱✱

If you can do these, pack your bags and join the circus.

THE 180

1

2

Start with a jump up, Ollie-style, then spin through half a circle and land going backward. What you do after that is anybody's guess. Probably safer just to slow down until you stop, if you haven't fallen off already.

Difficulty rating:
✳✳✳✳✳✳✳✳✳

THE 180-DEGREE REVERT

1

2

With your foot on the back brake, do the 180, but land as if you're doing a wheelie. Use your momentum to swivel around through another 180 degrees, bringing the front back down when you've completed the circle. Don't practice too long though—you'll end up dizzier than when you put your forehead on a broom handle and ran around it twenty times.

Difficulty rating: ✳✳✳✳✳✳✳✳

THE TAIL WHIP

1

Do an Ollie and simultaneously kick the rear of the scooter out with your back foot. It should spin around once beneath you like a helicopter blade before you land back on it. Until you perfect this high priest of the scooter stunt kingdom, practice by taking a step halfway through, lifting your foot up as the scooter boomerangs back. Advisable to wear shin pads for the first 428 attempts.

Difficulty rating: ✳✳✳✳✳✳✳✳✳✳

2

3

43

ME AND MY BABY

Three scooter fanatics tell us why their model is the best thing since the invention of the wheel.

WILLS AND HIS MICRO —A BRITISH PERSPECTIVE

I've got two Micros and one Know-Ped. I got my first Micro from Club Blue Room in London in March 2000. I went down to Brighton seafront to get the hang of it, and I've been riding it ever since. They're absolutely brilliant, so lightweight and dynamic. And when I'm not using it, I just fold it up and carry it over my shoulder.

I used to walk everywhere, but now I prefer the Micro. The Know-Ped is quite a lot bulkier and heavier, but that's still portable and comfortable to ride as well. Scooting's a brilliant sport and it does cut time. It used to take me ten minutes to walk from my door to the subway, now I can do it in three. I'm a host at the Millennium Dome in London, so I ride it around for work from zone to zone because the dome is so big. I spend about two hours a day on it. It can wear your leg out, but I don't really notice, as I'm used to walking. Sometimes I swap feet.

People think it's just a kids' thing—they remember having scooters when they were younger—but now it's for adults as well. These Micros, they're the urban soul's scooter, personal transport for the new millennium. You've got to be careful where you go, you can feel the roughness, but I think I've mastered most surfaces.

I've been down quite a few hills in Somerset, but you've got to be very careful because the wheels are quite small. I'm still working the tricks out. The only one I can do at the moment is to lift myself up and stick my feet forward. I've only fallen off once, but they are pretty easy to come off.

I got the extra scooters for my friends so that we can all go out together. I went to Paris last weekend with a friend and took the two Micros. People stared and asked questions—but you can buy them over there as well.

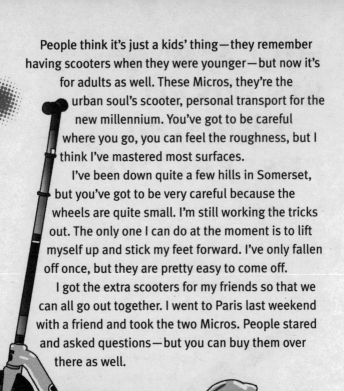

They're a huge craze all over the world at the moment. I'm going on holiday to Italy next month, so I'm going to take both scooters again. I might get a really bright yellow or orange one so that it really stands out.

Wills Gardner, 36, tourist guide at the Millennium Dome

JOE AND HIS K2 KICKBOARD— A WORLD TRAVELER

My Kickboard's lasted me more than a year now. I hate walking; that's why I bought it. I got it in August 1999 from Snow & Rock in Kensington, and I was the fifth person in London with one. Everyone was like, "What is that? Did you make it?" It's a pretty cool little device, still works well.

I bought it to go traveling with. My friend told me that Australia was really good for skating 'cause it's really smooth and flat—and it was such a savior, I was just speeding around everywhere. When I arrived, Micros had already caught on, but no one had seen a Kickboard before and they were amazed. Everyone who tried it said that it was totally better. It was a good talking point too; good for impressing the ladies.

The Kickboard's pretty low to the floor, so when you're pushing, you don't even have to bend your leg. That's why it's so much better than a skateboard—you can just cruise. It's a luxury way of traveling, but on those little Micros it's hard even to get two feet on it.

In Bali I took it on the boardwalk, and people would give me a tow on their mopeds. I met quite a few people just by having it. And it was excellent at airports because I had a suitcase with wheels. Airports are the best location—the floor's like marble, it's just saying, "Skate me."

Now I use my scooter to get to work. It's the best get-around thing. It takes about twenty minutes off my journey. It gives me more get-up-and-go in the mornings because I know that it won't be too traumatic getting to work. And I just laugh at all the people stuck in cars.

A bike is faster, a skateboard does more tricks, but the beauty of the scooter is that it folds up. On the scooter you're much more in control, and it's so quiet and smooth, people don't even hear you coming. The thing is, pedestrians don't walk in straight lines, especially when they've just woken up and they're going to work. So I'd put a little horn on it, a little *meep meep*, as I've run into the back of people when they've changed direction right in front of me.

I have hurt myself once. I tried to jump off a bandstand, and I landed it, but I took the weight on my knees and bent down. The joystick caught me in the ribs and that really hurt, but it didn't do any lasting damage.

I think to do really good tricks on it, to compete with the skateboard, they would need to change the design slightly because it's not very easy to pull off the ground. I can jump up a high step, but nothing higher than that, really. But my little brother here, Pod, he can jump on it and he's only six.

If I designed my own one, I'd put more bounce in it— maybe suspension in the front forks so that you could push your weight down and jump up. If there was spring in the handle, it would reduce the feeling of arthritis in your hands too, because it does vibrate a lot. And I'd change the grip. I think it should be a handle so that you could actually pull it up and get some serious air.

I'm planning to buy one of the new ones. The wheels are a lot bigger, so you'd be starting to compete with bikes, and it looks like it could do some serious concrete burning. Very nice construction. But with this one, I've got my money's worth, definitely.

Joe Plimmer, 24, photographer

ALICE AND HER SPORT GO-PED

I used to have a BMX when I was a kid and loved it. Then I tried my boyfriend's Go-Ped and I was addicted immediately. It takes a couple of tries to get used to, but you get the hang of it quite quickly. And it's so much fun.

I bought my own in May 1999 secondhand, which is cheaper. Mine's dark blue, but I want to spray it all pink and sparkly.

At weekends we go to the skate park or this really big deserted parking lot, which is good because it's got curbs that you can jump up onto and skid along. There's a whole group of us—four with Go-Peds, a couple with Monkey bikes, like miniature motorbikes, and some on BMXs.

I can do jumps, wheelies, and this trick where you put your stomach on the handlebars and stick your arms and legs out so you're in a star shape and keep on cruising. I'm trying to do a 180, but I keep stalling. I've seen people jumping over others lying down. You wouldn't catch me doing the lying down though! Loads of people I know have had accidents, just scrapes and bruises really. But I don't like to risk it. I'm not as much of a daredevil as they are.

I've bought extra suspension and an air

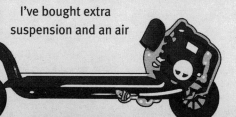

49

filter for it, a big chrome thing that makes the Go-Ped last longer and increases your speed, but I really got it because it's good for hooking your foot under so it's easier to do tricks. I've also got an underboard that fits beneath the scooter so you don't break it in two. And I wear a helmet. Mine's an Evel Knievel skaters' one.

We've taken them with us on vacation a few times. That's the handy thing about the Go-Ped—you can pick it up and take it everywhere. On one trip it was excellent because there was a really, really long path all the way along the beach, so we just bombed it up and down there.

> ❝I'm just on my way to meet a friend on my lunch hour. If I didn't have my scooter, I probably wouldn't bother, because it's too far to walk.❞
>
> *Sally, 23, Razor*

I think Razors are boring. You may as well walk. I like to go fast, to get somewhere quickly. I can get up to twenty-five miles per hour on my Go-Ped, and if I need exercise, I'll go to the gym. It's not heavy to carry around either; there's only a tiny engine. Actually, usually I just leave the motor running and walk along with it. It's very lazy, I know, but then that's why I got a scooter in the first place.

My dad sometimes goes on it, and he's fifty-three. All his friends absolutely love it. They're like, "Can we have a try?" It's just a big boy's toy. I bet I'll still be going around on it when I'm retired too, but by then everyone'll be floating around on hover scooters.

Alice Davies, 24, photo researcher

Scooter Fashion No-no's

What you *won't* be wearing this season!

* **Motorcycle helmet complete with visor** (we're surprised you got up the courage to leave the house)

* **Bell-bottoms/flares** (like having a couple of sails on your legs; you'll never build up any speed.)

* **Leg in a cast** (hobble home and eat some grapes)

* **Soccer cleats** (you may be late for practice, but you'll end up in the emergency room if you have to jump off.)

* **Galoshes** (that's not what we meant by burning rubber)

* **Umbrella** (leave it to Inspector Gadget)

* **High heels** (you'll take someone's eye out)

* **Cape/shawl** (you're not Batman, you know, and if the wind whips it up into your face, you'll be in trouble)

* **Tight skirt** (especially if you're a boy)

* **Hiker's backpack** (you'll be so top-heavy, you'll be pulling permanent wheelies)

51

CHANGING VROOMS

With so many scooters now on the streets, stand out from the pack by giving yours a makeover and adding some individual touches. Personalize your scooter by mixing and matching accessories, or do a little DIY to make it truly one of a kind. Then, when you've finished, why not give it a name? Go on, you know you want to.

ACCESSORIES

RAZOR

Replacement wheels come in various colors such as red, green, and blue. Or act like a Formula One star and make a pit stop when it rains to put on a spare set of black wet-weather wheels by Bridgestone. Even funkier are light wheels, which are transparent with red, white, and blue flashing LEDs. Get your in-lines on-line at **www.sharperimage.com; www.push-scooters.com.**

Rubber handlebar grips also come in different colors, from black, yellow, and red to transparent blue. Naturally, all are recyclable, as you'd expect from such an environmentally friendly product.

Other add-ons include a wheelie bar, which fits on the back and helps with tricks, knee-friendly suspension, colored shoulder straps, and motion-activated LED "brake" lights that simply slip into the two triangular holes at the back of the board. Carry everything around in your black nylon Razor bag, which folds up into a pouch to strap on your belt when you're on the move. And look out for a new Razor clothing line, coming soon for all you fashion heads.

GO-PED

Find cool designer decks at **www.goped.com; www.crosswinds.net/~gopedservice.**
Bad boys should try the X-Ped, which is a stunt machine, while speed freaks will be attracted to the Hoverboard, which is the lightest and fastest of all the models.

KICKBOARD

Swap your treads for some extra-wide downhill slick tires for added speed, or pneumatic rubber off-road wheels to give those bumps short shrift. You can even buy locks, bags and, for suckerlike grip, special sneakers with an air heel and boarder sole. Check out **www.razorkickboardscooters.com**

CUSTOMIZING

The only limit here is your own imagination. In Japan, where there are entire magazines devoted to scooters, you'll never see the same machine twice. "A Japanese cowboy came in once, she was like Tonto," says Ashley Larkman from the skate shop Club Blue Room in London. "She had a huge cowboy hat, a shirt with all the tassles, and cowboy boots with spurs, and her scooter had all these fluffy mascots and lights on the handlebars. She had a finger bell on it too, and you could hear her coming down the street—*Ding-ding, ding-ding*. We'd be like, 'Here she comes again.'"

Don't let them have all the fun—get in on the act with these top tips.

GRIP TAPE

Not only does it look cool, but it'll help you with tricks, because when you stick it onto your board, it'll give you extra . . . well . . . grip. The plain black variety looks a little like sandpaper and comes in rolls, which you can then cut up as you please to make your own patterns. Or buy special logo strips—there are thousands of skate-type designs, so there's something for everyone. Check out any skate shop.

STICKERS

Slap 'em on anywhere except the wheels, where they'll
come off in the rain. Scour toy shops for your favorite
characters from TV or the big screen, or try the Internet.
Sites such as **www.stickemup.com** have cool
skateboardy designs and retro fireball stickers from the
1970s, which can be ordered on-line. Even better, if
you're a computer whiz, you can create your own styles
on a PC—maybe try writing your own name in a funky
design—and then take the disc into a copy shop, and
tell them what colors and materials you want, and a few
hours later you'll get your eager hands on your very
own personalized sticker.

STOMP PADS

These are little metal or plastic devices that
snowboarders use for grip when they climb off the ski
lift and back onto the board. You can just as easily stick
them onto your scooter, either to help with tricks or just
to make it look cool. They come in all shapes and
designs, are about four inches wide, and can be bought
from snowboard and outdoor-gear shops.

ANODIZING

For seriously cool customizers only. Anodizing is a
complex scientific process that you might remember
from chemistry class. But all you need to know is that it
permanently changes the color of the metal on your
scooter, unlike paint, which can chip off. Just take your
scooter into any metalworking joint and tell them what
you want. You can dye the whole scooter—make it gold,
brass, sparkly blue, whatever—or take it apart and just
do a few nuts and bolts. Either way, you'll be the envy of
all your friends.

scooting stars

**Find out whether you were
born to ride with these
special horoscopes.**

Aries–The Ram
March 21–April 19

Adventurous and full of energy, the ram is the first to get in on any craze, the scooter being no exception. You're a real daredevil and love big challenges. Energetic Arians will try anything once, including the most complicated tricks—hey, who cares about bumps and bruises when you're having fun?
Top tip: Stay safe and wear protective gear.

Taurus–The Bull
April 20–May 20

You were born to ride and are never happier than when scooting through your local park among the trees and flowers. Scooting is right up your garden path because it doesn't harm the environment. Practical and down-to-earth, you prefer straightforward scooting from A to B rather than showing off with fancy footwork. Don't just plough through those potholes, though—remember to go around them.
Top tip: Take the bull by the horns. Be adventurous and try something new.

Gemini–The Twins
May 21–June 20

You're quite restless and can easily lose your concentration. As a result, you find it difficult to master new moves and tend to give up if it doesn't come easy the first time. This may have something to do with the two sides of your personality battling with each other. At least you shouldn't have any problems remembering to swap your feet.
Top tip: Keep at it—practice makes perfect.

Cancer—The Crab
June 21–July 22

You're an emotional type and can be very sensitive. If anyone should make a snide remark about your scooting style, like the crab, you will retreat into your shell and sulk for days. But when you're in a better mood, people find you kind and caring, and always the first to help other scooter maniacs.

Top tip: Remember to go forward, not just sideways.

Leo—The Lion
July 23–August 22

You're the king of the urban jungle. Like the lion himself, you love being the leader of the pack, and you'll usually be found scooting along in front of your friends. You tend to be the one who decides where to go and what to do, and your friends naturally follow you. You've also got a big heart and will be first to the scene to help if someone takes a nosedive.

Top tip: Don't get too bossy with your posse!

Virgo—The Virgin
August 23–September 22

You're a complete perfectionist who spends hours making sure your scooter retains that fresh-from-the-box appearance. You keep it so clean you can see your Puma Sprints' reflection in the board. You wouldn't be seen dead without all the right gear, and you practice all your moves in private—no one is allowed to watch you until you're 100 percent accurate.

Top tip: Relax and don't be afraid to make mistakes.

Libra—The Balance
September 23–October 22

If scooter rage breaks out, you'll usually find a Libran trying to settle the argument fairly. Librans have a very strong sense of justice and love peace and harmony in their lives. They also love beauty and are attracted to the sleekest, most expensive scooters. Should have no problems with balance, either.

Top tip: Looks aren't everything, so forget appearances and focus on fun.

Scorpio—The Scorpion
October 23–November 21

You're prone to jealousy and may find yourself sizing up other people's scooters, especially if they've got the latest Razor Double Air Flextastic Super-Pro. Possessions are very important to you, and you get attached to special things very easily. Once you've got yourself a shiny new scooter, you won't let it out of your sight.

Top tip: Let your friends have a turn occasionally.

Sagittarius—The Archer
November 22–December 21

You love a challenge, and if you're a typical Sag, you can be found trying things like 720-degree double backflips—tricks no one else has ever heard of, let alone attempted. You love to joke around and don't take yourself too seriously—which is just as well, since you're always falling off in public places. Doh!

Top tip: Look where you're going.

Capricorn–The Goat
December 22–January 19

You're a sensible mountain biker who's been slowly filling up the piggy bank for months, saving for the scooter of your dreams. Once you've got it in your sweaty little hands, you'll spend all your spare time perfecting your basic technique before going anywhere near an "Ollie," or whatever it is those other kids call them. You're a stickler for getting things right.

Top tip: Throw caution to the wind and try some of the tricks in this book—you might actually enjoy them!

Aquarius–The Water Bearer
January 20–February 18

Bright, bold Aquarians love new ideas, and you were probably one of the first people in your area to get a scooter. Independent and strong-willed, you prefer to go out scooting on your own rather than with a group.

Top tip: Try being more sociable. And avoid those puddles, water lover. You'll take a spill.

Pisces–The Fishes
February 19–March 20

Dreamy Pisceans are usually off with the fishes and enjoy scooting around at their own pace, just going with the flow in their own little world. The Pisces sign rules the feet, and as a result you are capable of some pretty nifty little moves—you should be a whiz at the Tail Whip in particular—so long as you can put your mind to it.

Top tip: Stay alert and snap out of your daydream, otherwise you'll go straight into the back of that pedestrian.

SCOOTER RAGE

Snippets of sidewalk sour Grapes

✖ "What time's your mom expecting you home for dinner?"

✖ "Get off the pavement."

✖ "It's Hopalong Cassidy."

✖ "Watch out for the lamppos—oh, too late."

✖ "Any slower and you'll be going backward."

✖ "What's your other scooter, a Porsche?"

✖ "Just take the bus like everyone else."

✖ "Aaaaaaaaaaaargh!"

The Inventor

"I created the scooter because I was too lazy to walk to my favorite sausage place."

Scooter inventor Wim Ouboter is well on his way to becoming a millionaire—just from being lazy. The forty-year-old former Swiss banker designed his first scooter in 1994 because he couldn't be bothered to walk twenty minutes to get takeout. Now the craze has spiraled so much that he's talking about it becoming an Olympic sport.

"I created the scooter because I was too lazy to walk to my favorite sausage place, the Star Grill," he admits. "It was one of these awkward distances and I thought there had to be something that you could take out of your closet, put under your arm, and go."

So he set about building a contraption that would ease the rumbles in his stomach. Over the next two weekends he built his first prototype scooter, using in-line skate wheels and an old bike column. But things didn't go quite according to plan. "It worked, but people were laughing at me in the street," he says. "Everyone thought I was crazy—even some of my closest friends."

> **"I can do jumps and wheelies. I fell over once and hurt my knee, but it's not difficult. You just get on them and scoot around."**
> *Jack, 10, Razor*

Disappointed, Wim abandoned the scooter in his garage for three years and forgot about it. But fortunately for us, the local kids didn't. "While I was at work, the children from my neighborhood saw the scooter and would ask my wife if they could have a ride. Sometimes there were sixteen kids waiting for their turn. My wife said, 'There's something about this scooter, you need to take it seriously.'"

So he went back to the drawing board, put some more of his own money in, and came up with a more lightweight and stylish model—the Razor. After numerous failed attempts to get financing, he finally found a manufacturer in Taiwan prepared to gamble on his machine. Today his Taiwanese partner employs six thousand people in three factories in China, churning out fifty thousand Razors per day.

Wim had always known that scooters were fun—he'd been riding one since he was five. His parents had bought him and his two sisters scooters because one sister was born with one leg shorter than the other and couldn't ride a bike. But he had no idea how popular they would become.

"I was not expecting so many people from five to seventy to be using scooters," says Wim, who these days zips around on the Kickboard and the new razor Air Flex. "But they're very easy to use—in-line skates are a little more complicated and riding a bike is not as much fun."

Now all his critics have stopped laughing, and many of them are trying to copy his idea. Of the 100,000 scooters sold in Hong Kong in recent months, around 70 percent were Razor knockoffs. "They're even copying our name," moans Wim. "But my father said once, 'If you get copied, it's a compliment, because you've got a good product.'"

Proud to be doing his bit for Switzerland, Wim still runs his worldwide scooter empire with just five staff from a two-bedroom apartment in Zurich. "Hopefully we're getting away from our image of just making chocolate, watches, and Swiss army knives," he says. "Scooters are not a fad. This is just the beginning of the century of Razor mobility. It's not a joke anymore. People really believe in the future of the scooter."

If the pavement is too bumpy, it feels a bit like holding a pneumatic drill, but on smooth surfaces you can get it up to a good speed, at least as fast as an average run. I fell off once when I was going down a hill too quickly. But apart from that I've had no real accidents.

Polly, 26, Razor

Places NOT to Go on a Scooter

* **The Tour de France** (King of the Mountains? We think not.)

* **An expedition to Everest** (it'd be great for getting down again, but there's "snow" way you'd make it to the top!)

* **The countryside** (especially anywhere with cattle herds—or cow patties . . .)

* **An army base** (left, left, left, right . . . aaargh! Saluting could cause a few problems too.)

* **The Sahara desert** (you won't be able to get much momentum)

* **A car wash** (even more so if you're ticklish)

* **The supermarket** (do you really think those eggs are going to make it back in one piece?)

* **Bungee jumping** (somehow we don't think you'd be able to stay on the scooter)

* **The Eiffel Tower** (too many steps, and they're all full of holes)

* **A tightrope** (c'mon, you're not *that* good)

The Whiz Kid

"I built my first Web site when I was ten and bought my first stocks and shares a year later."

Most of us see a scooter and think fun: Dominic McVey thinks business. While other kids his age are out in the park racing one another and doing stunts, fifteen-year-old Dominic is locked up at home in his bedroom on his computer, running his own Internet business. He brings scooters over to Europe from America, earning more money than he could ever possibly fit in his pocket.

Scooter Boy, as he's affectionately known in the papers, runs the company Scooter U.K., which ships motorized and push scooters over the Atlantic, and it's made him into Europe's youngest self-made millionaire.

"I built my first Web site when I was ten and bought my first stocks and shares a year later," says Dominic. He then began importing gadgets like minidiscs, MP3 players, and portable hi-fis from Japan that you couldn't buy in the U.K. for family friends, as well as organizing end-of-term parties at school, selling tickets for £5 a pop.

Together with birthday and Christmas money he managed to raise £3,000 to set up his scooter business. When he sent an E-mail to Viza Motors asking to be their U.K. distributor, he didn't mention he was only fourteen. "I didn't think it was necessary," he says. "I thought scooters were ideal for everyone in Britain, as traffic problems were getting so bad, and I knew I could do a good job. I wouldn't say I foresaw the scooter craze, but I was determined to set one in effect."

Now his weekly turnover is heading toward a staggering £15 million as he deals with fourteen countries throughout Europe, and his Web site

> **"It's just convenience for me. It takes me ten minutes to get to work, compared with half an hour by subway."**
> *Fumihito, 27, Razor*

(**www.scooters-uk.co.uk**) receives thirty thousand hits a day. Yet Dominic still runs his business entirely on his own, and somehow finds time for his studies at Forest School in Snaresbrook, London.

Surely he's the most popular guy in school. "I don't like to say yes. I try to be modest. But quite possibly."

And what about girls? "Well, there's none on the agenda, but I'm sure there's a few that would like to be." One thing's for sure—he shouldn't have any problems with business studies. "I'm not sure how to approach my teacher anymore," admits Dominic. "Most of the time he doesn't know what I'm talking about.

"If I didn't have to sleep, I would be working on the business twenty-four hours a day, seven days a week. I find it fun. Instead of sitting at home playing games, I get on the phone, meet new people, make new contacts, maintain Web sites. I do go out with my friends, but I have to sacrifice a lot. I've got the rest of my life to live. If this is a nice earner, I don't have to worry about the future."

> **"**It's quite difficult, because you have to learn your balance—don't use the brake first, because you might fall over a lot. I fell over once when there were bumps and cracks and things in the pavement. You go in one of those and it flips you. But you can watch people on the street and learn from them, because it's not that hard.**"**
>
> *Antonia, 11, Razor*

Right now all Dominic can think about is his latest push scooter, the Viza Kikit, which he believes will outsell the Micro. It's got six-inch pneumatic tires and minispoke wheels, a wider deck for more foot room, a different folding mechanism, and LED lights in the wheels ("It looks as if it's got fire coming out the back"), and it weighs just under eight pounds.

"Yesterday I went out on it in London, and I had kids running up to me, touching it, saying, 'Where did you get that? Look at those wheels, they're amazing.' I was racing someone around town, and they're so much faster—with one push they have to do five. One of their dads was even offering me money for it."

Dominic's also planning to organize a scooting world championship, with the finals to take place in America. He's also got ambitions to be a television presenter and is developing yet more Web sites, not at all scooter related, but he won't reveal any details right now. "Some people say I'm the next Richard Branson [chairman of Virgin]—and that would be nice. I'll be disappointed if it doesn't happen, but it won't be the end of the world."

> **"Ever since I purchased it, I have become the coolest dude in town. It was one of those things I saw in the window and said, 'This thing looks damn cool and loads of fun.' The next time I went to the shop, it was mine, done deal."**
> *Aaron, 26, Razor*

69

The Record Breaker

"It will be one of
the hardest things
I've ever done."

F eeling a little sore after a little jaunt to the park on your scooter? Think of twenty-eight-year-old Matt Perry from Burnley, England. He's setting off to scoot from New York to San Francisco on a Razor— that's a distance of approximately three thousand miles straight across the middle of America by push power alone. All in the name of charity, of course.

"I'm going to spend pretty much every day on the road, and I estimate it'll take about three weeks if I average around fifteen miles an hour," says Matt, a marketeer for an Internet company. "I'll be scooting nine hours a day—a full day's work." Not everyone's idea of a day at the office.

But then Matt's used to it. He already holds the world record for the longest distance covered in twenty-four hours on a push scooter—161 miles, set on an athletic track in Lancashire, England, beating the previous record of 150 miles held by Nashrita Fuhrmann from New Jersey.

He also traveled from John o'Groat's, Scotland, to Land's End, England, on a Veriflex scooter in 1996, again for charity. Matt completed the trip in five weeks in one piece, even if his right sneaker didn't. Despite having hardly ever scooted before (he says he had a "deprived youth"), he was determined to do the trip in a way that had never been attempted.

> "I bought it to get a little exercise—it works the upper thigh muscle—and save money on subway fares at the same time. Watch out for potholes, though. I didn't see that tiny one and went straight over the handlebars!"
> *Claire, 20, Razor*

"I'd already decided that I was going to do the journey, and then just as I was thinking about it, this kid went past me on a push scooter," he says. "I just thought, 'There's an idea.'" After completing the trip, he was hooked. Two years later he was at it again, shadowing the first leg of the Tour de France, from Dublin to Cork. "I was the only person on a push scooter among thousands of cyclists. I was scooting through the night, keeping one step ahead, just following the route."

This time around, he's going to be the star of the show. The *Guinness Book of World Records* people have been notified about his American jaunt, and he's going to be filmed before setting off by BBC's *Record Breakers*. Plus, he's going to be using a scooter with much smaller wheels than the ones he's ridden in the past.

"It will be a challenge, there's no two ways about it," says Matt. "It will be one of the hardest things I've ever done. I've got to battle against all the elements, the extreme weather conditions. . . . Anything could happen, but I'm still confident I'll do it."

He's certainly making sure that he's fully prepared, getting up at six in the morning every day of the week except Sunday to do an hour's training—running and a five-mile scoot—before work. Plus in the evenings he practices capoeira, a bizarre yet beautiful Brazilian martial art that's a cross between fighting and dancing and is great for improving your balance.

But even with all the training in the world, most people still think he's crazy to attempt to cross the good ole U.S. of A. on a push scooter. "I do regard myself as quite an eccentric character," concedes Matt. "But I think scooters are an ideal way to promote green alternative travel. And they're really fun too. They're very liberating—you can be a kid on the scooter."

Stuff
You'll find in a
Scooter Maniac's
Backpack

- **✳** City street map
- **✿** **Bandages for skinned knees**
- **✳** Cell phone (so you can keep up with the news wherever you are)
- **✿** ***Tony Hawk's Pro Skater 2* PlayStation game**
- **✳** Other grown-up toys, such as a Palm Pilot and a Pokémon Game Boy
- **✿** **WD-40**
- **✳** Bottle of mineral water and a healthy snack bar (anything nutritious and loaded with energy)
- **✿** **Photos of you on your scooter in exotic locations (outside the Taj Mahal, in front of the Pyramids, etc.)**
- **✳** Sunblock and lip balm (you tan easier in the breeze, you know)
- **✿** **Money (for bus fare in case you can't be bothered to scoot home again)**

The Wheel Story

They don't just grow on trees, you know.

Scooters have traveled a long way since kids used to make their own by nailing a pair of roller skates to a piece of a milk crate way back in the 1930s. They are the latest in a long line of multi-wheeled machines that are just as much fun to play with as they are useful for transportation—from roller skates, in-line skates, skateboards, snakeboards, longboards, and BMXs to those ridiculous lie-down bikes. But no other machine is going to have a bigger impact at the start of the new millennium.

The first scooter was invented in Germany in 1816, but it wasn't until the 1950s that kids really got into them. Families were moving out of the inner city into bigger houses on the outskirts, so there was more space for children to play in. Scooters became a big hit in the suburbs, but these old-fashioned models were nothing like the sleek machines you see today. On these clunky wooden contraptions you wouldn't have dared try a trick—it was hard enough just to go in a straight line.

Over the years the scooter remained popular, but in the late 1980s in-line skating and skateboarding became the trendy way to cruise. The scooter all but disappeared. The Scootech or Ninja scooter, a scooter with BMX brakes, handlebars, and wheels twice the size of today's models, made a final attempt to recapture the dying scooter craze in the early nineties, but to no avail.

It wasn't until the summer of 1999, when the first batch of twenty thousand Razors went on sale in Japan and sold out to eager teens within weeks, that the humble scooter got its foot back in the door. Inventor Wim Ouboter says, "It was perfect because the Japanese like everything that's high-tech.

"Also the subway system in Japan is pretty crowded, so if you try to take a foldable bicycle on there, you'll probably get knocked down because you take up too much room. But with the Razor there was no problem. That's why it was so successful." He's not joking— today 75,000 scooters are sold each week in Japan.

Soon Razors had moved across the Pacific and rolled over Australia in the same way as they had Japan. In the streets of Sydney they were everywhere. But when the Razors arrived in Britain last October, they weren't such an instant hit as they had been on the other side of the world. "It took a while to kick off here because English people are wary of new trends," explains Ashley Larkman, a manager at Club Blue Room in London.

"I've owned one since Christmas, and since then I have convinced at least twelve other kids aged ten to thirteen to buy one. We have made scooter business cards and started a club. My friends and I have got quite good at performing."
Adam, 11, Razor

However, the Razors were soon picked up by the "big kids"—twenty- to twenty-five-year-olds—and they began getting noticed on the streets. "Once they were starting to be seen around a bit, people were like, 'Oh, that's cool actually, I don't mind it,'" says Ashley. "Now every time you turn a corner, you see one."

"I'm a skateboarder really, but it's fun on these things."
Jamie, 24, Razor

Scooters became such a hit in big cities like London partly because they were used by adults who saw them as ideal for commuting to work—a way of avoiding rush-hour traffic. But also because the first people to ride and sell them were so cool, the scooter became a fashion statement.

Since London is seen as one of the style capitals of the world, before long everyone else wanted a piece of the action. "We had people coming in from everywhere around the globe, saying, 'We've never seen these before, these are incredible,'" says Ashley. "Americans loved them. But the biggest fans were the northern Europeans—they'd come in and take five back for their kids."

The Razor is now the highest-selling item in many sports and toy shops. Most stores report that they are selling out of scooters as fast as they can stock them. But you won't find them only in specialty stores—you can now pick up scooters in almost any mall. In the U.K. they're scooting off the shelves at a rate of around fifteen thousand a week.

Across the Atlantic world domination continued when the Razors first arrived in the U.S. after being tested in the most trend-obsessed state of them all, Hawaii, where their arrival signaled "mob scenes" in February 2000. They then migrated to the West Coast of America and again proved a success with skate dudes and businessmen alike.

> **"I first saw the Razor in Australia and thought, I have to get one of those. Ever since I have had more fun than I ever had riding a skateboard. People always ask me, 'What is that thing?' while I am carrying it in the collapsed position. They are all surprised it is a scooter."**
>
> ***Sean, 25, Razor***

But the West Coast surfer kids in particular already had their hands full with their very own type of scooter, the gas-powered Go-Ped. All the way back in 1985, Go-Ped founder and inventor Steve Patmont formed family business Patmont Motor Werks in California to develop and produce his motorized machines. By 1989 he was doing so well that he had to move out of his garage factory. Two years later Go-Peds caught on in the extreme-sports world and kids started to race them.

In the mid-nineties Steve invented Go-Ped's first nonmotorized model, the Know-Ped, and fueled by the buzz surrounding the Razor, demand for all types of Go-Peds started to shoot off the skate ramp. "Our sales have doubled over the year before," says Steve. "We can't meet demand."

> **"At first I felt very silly, but now I try to concentrate on avoiding potholes. You can go pretty fast when you've got a clear way downhill."**
> *Guy, 35, Razor*

At San Francisco gadget emporium the Sharper Image, the first store to sell the scooters in the U.S., the Razor broke records in three months to become the best-selling item the company had. "It's the hottest product we have ever seen," says marketing chief Tony Farrell. "It's the skateboard for people who can't skateboard."

This new "skateboard" has now become the top-selling sporting goods product in America, and the scooter love affair is heading north into Canada.

> **"You don't have to sit down and take them off, like with Rollerblades. It really is practical."**
> *Yilmaz, 23, Razor*

Meanwhile, in Europe, Razors are selling well in Switzerland, Germany, Austria, Italy, Spain, and France. It seems the whole world is going nuts with two-wheeled craziness. Scooter mania has truly gone global.

DID YOU KNOW ... ?

* **German members of Parliament use Razors to save time getting around their huge new parliament building.**

    * **The most famous scooter film is called *Return of the Pedi*—a half-hour joyride of Go-Ped stunts set to a cool soundtrack.**

* **Fashion designer Alexander McQueen came out to cheering crowds on a Kickboard after the end of his London Fashion Week show.**

    * **The Razor is known as the Micro in Europe.**

* **The French call the push scooter *trottinette*, from *trottoir* (pavement).**

    * **There is a band called Scooter. They're a hard house trio from Hamburg, Germany.**

✱ The world speed record on a Razor is 110 km/hour (downhill), set by Juerg Zackmann in August 2000. The forty-year-old stuntman and hairdresser was later stopped by the police while trying to break his own record.

✱ Offical timekeepers at the Sydney Olympics were issued with Kickboards so that they could get to their races in plenty of time.

✱ In Japan more than 1.2 million scooters have been sold already.

✱ One wealthy customer in London bought a Razor for puttering around his huge mansion.

✱ Department store giant Wal-Mart has ordered three million Razors to sell in its chain of stores.

✱ Using a scooter, you burn up at least 300 calories an hour—the equivalent of a Mars bar.

✱ A seventy-year-old Dutch lady bought a Razor while on vacation in London in order to keep up with her scooting grandkids.

To Infinity and Beyond

NEW MODELS

The two new models from the Razor stable are the Air and the Air Flex. Both have all the features of the Razor-130 A1, such as front suspension, a wheelie bar, and rear LED flashing lights, but the Air has larger pneumatic tires for a smoother ride, while the Air Flex has—surprise, surprise—a flexible board too. Further down the line inventor Wim Ouboter's got something a little bit special up his sleeve. "We're developing an ABS brake system [used in cars] and a tiny electric engine. The idea is that you push up to five kilometers an hour and then the engine kicks in automatically. It's not for uphill, it's just a really light scooter because it still has to be portable. Our goal is that it should not weigh more than seven kilos."

"I bought one last week in Sydney and brought it home for my children here in South Africa. Brilliant."
Steve, 36, Razor

K2 has also just brought out four new types of Kickboard:

- the Kick Two, which has a more sophisticated steering system
- the Cross Kick, an off-road beast with larger pneumatic tires
- the Absolute Kick, with fast slick tires and a superwide back wheel for better grip at high speeds
- the Carveboard, the ace in the pack, a four-wheeled beauty (the two wheels at the front are the larger this time) with a sloping board and a supersensitive turning mechanism that kicks in at the slightest tilt

Best of all, prices have come down to street level too.

Our tip: You can already buy longboards with built-in electric panels that display start and stop times, date, speed, and the distance you've traveled. Surely it's only a matter of time before similar devices start appearing on scooter handlebars.

> **"**I use it to keep up with Dad. He walks too fast.**"**
> *Samantha, 9, Razor*

INTO THE FUTURE

With a whole shopping cart of new machines coming on the market, scooter mania shows no signs of slowing down. "Snowboarding and Rollerblading were supposed to be fads too," says Joseph De La Jara, vice president of marketing at DLJ International, one of the two major U.S. distributors for the Razor. "Today they are still multimillion-dollar businesses."

Skateboards have been around for more than thirty years now, so it looks like it shouldn't be too bumpy a ride for scooters, especially with those new pneumatic tires. Owning a scooter is like owning a bike—once you've bought one, it's always going to be part of your life. And with governments promising to build an ever more extensive network of bicycle paths, scooting is only going to get easier.

> **"**I ride them to school. It's much easier than walking. I can go very fast, but you have to change feet 'cause the foot you stand on gets tired easily.**"**
> *Sam, 10, Razor*

The scooter craze will get another push in the right direction as it becomes recognized as an international sport in the same way as skateboarding. The first scooting world championships have already taken place—in Zurich, Switzerland, in September 2000—with speed, slalom, and freestyle events, sponsored by multinational companies such as Ericsson and Swatch. Competitions are also planned in England, Germany, and France.

Meanwhile, downhill Kickboard racing is a serious sport in Holland. Contestants use special slick tires and collapse the steering column, crouching down to avoid wind resistance. The Dutch Autoped Federation has been organizing its own races since as far back as 1986, mainly for Kickbikes, but more recently for any form of foot-powered vehicle.

> **"I received mine as a gift four weeks ago. I took my two kids to ride them down to the beach. I was stopped twenty-one times and asked where I got [the scooters] from and how much they cost."**
> *John, 37, Razor*

At the same time, scooters are going to become even more accessible to the general public. During the Olympics scooter rental stations were installed around Sydney, where footsore spectators could hire out a machine for a small fee, returning it to the closest station at the end of the day.

A similar scheme has already been implemented in Berlin. Plans are also afoot to really take advantage of those supersmooth floors and introduce scooters to airports for that last-minute dash to the departure gate. And surely it can only be a matter of time before Sony brings out a scooting game for PlayStation.

> **"You can really hot-dog on this thing. Plus, I feel safe because one foot is on the ground, which is the important thing."**
> *Kaarin, 22, Kickbike*

So, what's going to be the next craze? Hovering boards? Jet-propelled backpacks? Motorized sneakers? Who knows? But the latest fad to come out of the U.S. is something you couldn't even make up—dog scooting. It's the ultimate slacker's method for exercising your furry friend—forget pushing, you just stand on the scooter while Fido pulls you along.

"To dog scooter, you need a dog who likes to run, a harness, a tug line, and a scooter," says Daphne Lewis. "Scooting after a running dog is more fun than walking with a dog on a leash." If you don't believe us, read her book, *My Dog Likes to Run, I Like to Ride*.

Are You a Scooter Maniac?

Do you know your Bunny Hops from your Bonuses? Your Ollies from your Wheelies? Try this fun quiz to find out whether you're a genius or a dunce at the School of Scooter Skills.

1. After your very first ride on a scooter you could just about manage:

a. A couple of Tail Whips and a One-Foot Air—no problem.

b. After hours of practice, an Ollie to be proud of.

c. To get off the scooter without bashing your shins with the board.

2. You can tell your scooter from everyone else's because:

a. It's got stunt pegs on the front wheels and your name stuck on the board in reflective vinyl lettering.

b. It's super shiny, well oiled, and given lots of tender loving care.

c. Uh, I'm just trying to remember where I left it.

3. You hit a hole and fly off your scooter in front of everyone. Do you:

a. Do a quick backflip to land back on your machine, moving swiftly into a dramatic 180-Degree Revert? Hey, it's a trick no one's ever seen before (and aren't ever likely to again).

b. Pretend you're limbering up for a Crouch—always best to practice on dry land, you know?

c. Scoot off as fast as your one little leg will take you?

4. At night you toss and turn, dreaming about being:

a. The boss of a top international scooter company.

b. The owner of a brand-new Carveboard.

c. Wrapped up in bandages.

5. A Cherry Picker is:

a. A piece of cake.

b. Tricky, but you're getting there.

c. Someone who sells fruit for a living.

6. When you're out scooting, other people usually:

a. Gather around you, clapping and whooping at your incredible array of stunts.

b. Don't take much notice (unless you bump into them, silly).

c. Point at you and fall over laughing.

7. Before the scooter craze happened, you:

a. Were a complete skateboard freak.

b. Sometimes went in-line skating.

c. Lounged around on the sofa in front of the TV (nothing much has changed, then).

8. Finish the following sentence: "I need my scooter because . . ."

a. My life wouldn't be complete without it.

b. It's the most fun you can have on two wheels.

c. My bike got stolen last year.

Turn the page to see how you scored!

Report Card

Count up your score to see how many *A*'s, *B*'s or *C*'s you got.

Mostly *A*'s

You are one *serious* scooter maniac. Cool and collected, especially when under pressure, you were able to scoot before you could walk (hey, you only need one leg, after all), and you're only truly happy when you're on wheels. In fact, you've already got another couple of subjects under your belt—having got top marks in both skateboarding and in-line skating. There's no doubt that you've polished up on each and every trick in the book, and let's face it, you're something of a scooting know-it-all. The thing is, you find it all "wheelie" easy! An asset to any scooting school.

Mostly *B*'s

As far as scooting goes, you're a solid B student. You're having a wicked time with your new speciality but don't take it *too* seriously. You've got plenty of potential and can turn it on for exam situations, but you're happy either to leave the superadvanced stuff to the real pros or to copy their stunts at your desk with your finger skateboard when no one's looking. After all, it's not just about learning, but hanging out with your friends and having a good time. A little bit more concentration and you should do well in the future.

Mostly *C*'s

Oh, dear. You're really not applying yourself. When it comes to scooting, you're taking one step forward and two steps backward. You lack so much motivation, we really wonder why you bother turning up with the scooter at all—perhaps your parents are forcing you to make an effort because they've spent so much money on your scooting education. One thing's for sure, you were sitting at the back of the class paying so little attention to what was going on around you that this craze has really got you in a spin. Unless you get some stabilizers, we think it might be better if you stayed at home from now on. You're disrupting the others.

Keep on scooting!